PAUL E. MILLER'S
A PRAYING LIFE
DISCUSSION GUIDE

BY COURTNEY MILLER SNEED &
CYNDI ANDERSON

Interactive Bible Studies for Small Groups

For Dad, who showed me how to pray in the desert—C.M.S.
For Lanning, who has encouraged me with his gracious support
and faith-filled prayers—C.A.

seeJesus
PO Box 197
Telford, PA 18969
215.721.3113
www.seeJesus.net

The vision of seeJesus is a transformed church that reflects the beauty of Jesus. Our mission is to create high quality interactive Bible studies and training for small groups and outreach.

Scripture quotations are from The Holy Bible, English Standard Version, copyright ©2001 by Crossway Bibles, a division of Good News Publishers. Used by permission. All rights reserved.

All other quotations are from *A Praying Life* by Paul Miller, ©2009 Paul Miller. NavPress: Colorado Springs, CO, 2009.

Cover Design: Carol Smith
Interior Design & Layout: Courtney Sneed
Editor: Lydia Erin Allums

ISBN-10: 0-9844964-0-8
ISBN-13: 978-0-9844964-0-2

Printed in the United States of America

CONTENTS

FOREWORD

Just over ten years ago, Paul Miller came to the northwest suburbs of Chicago, Illinois to share the rudiments of a seminar on prayer that he had recently written. A handful of us gathered in a friend's basement to see and experience the very earliest layout of the seminar that is now known to thousands of people simply as PrayerLife. It was one of the most exhilarating experiences of my entire Christian life. I knew from that Saturday forward, I would never be the same.

I was not disappointed. Up until that time, prayer was simply one of many important disciplines in the life of the Christian—but I was not very good at it. My struggles with prayer won the day and I fell, as so many do, into a busy life that was essentially prayerless. And I felt it; the Christian life had become a chore rather than a vital relationship. After going through the course and incorporating the ideas, I have found the surprising wonder of doing life the way Jesus did, by constant prayer with the Father. Jesus really did live his earthly life by constantly interrupting his Father, knowing his Father delighted in his doing so. Following this same pattern has made the Christian life thrilling for me and many of those who have gone through the PrayerLife course.

Since that time in the basement ten years ago, Paul and I have presented the PrayerLife course in a variety of conferences, seminars, and retreats, to thousands of people both in the United States and abroad. When one gives a seminar many times, opportunities for refinement abound. After times of constant refining, often after each seminar, the book *A Praying Life* was ready to be born.

It became obvious that God was going to bless the book the way he had been blessing the PrayerLife course in the past ten years. Within hours, the entire first printing of the book had sold out. As word of mouth about the book spread throughout different faith group networks, calls to our seeJesus ministry office began to multiply quickly. People were asking for a Discussion Guide/Leader's Guide so groups of friends could go through the book together. Courtney Miller Sneed, with the help of Cyndi Anderson, worked tirelessly to produce this invaluable resource that you now have in your hands. The church will forever be indebted to the two of them for bringing together such a great tool.

Whether you have read *A Praying Life* and now want to go through it with a group of friends, or you have been through the PrayerLife course and want to follow it up with the book and this Discussion/Leader's Guide, we wish you the same exhilaration as you learn to pray.

—Bob Allums, Director of PrayerLife Ministries, seeJesus

Introduction

Paul Miller writes in *A Praying Life*, "When Jesus describes the intimacy he wants with us, he talks about joining us for dinner" (p. 20). A companion to *A Praying Life*, this discussion guide is meant to help you set aside your distractions, and show up for dinner excited. We know that doesn't all happen at once, and we mean to walk with you in the process. Each chapter in this guide corresponds with a chapter from *A Praying Life*. Through asking questions this guide compels you to flesh out Paul's teaching into the nitty-gritty of your life, freeing the real you to meet with your Father who loves you.

While *A Praying Life* can be personally applied, we believe it was made to study with others. The value of wrestling with it alongside other struggling "pray-ers" cannot be overstated. You will find yourself reaping benefits as you give yourself to the process. Studying it in community will open up new insights, and help you to grow integrity and joy as you (re)learn to pray.

A Leader's Guide is included at the end, and organized according to two reading schedules: a 13 week schedule and an 18 week schedule. Choose the schedule that works best for you.

Enjoy the feast before you. He is waiting!

—Courtney Miller Sneed & Cyndi Anderson

13 WEEK READING SCHEDULE

Week 1...... Chapters 1-2
Week 2...... Chapters 3-5
Week 3...... Chapters 6-8
Week 4...... Chapters 9-11
Week 5...... Chapters 12-14
Week 6...... Chapters 15-17
Week 7...... Chapters 18-20
Week 8...... Chapters 21-22
Week 9...... Chapters 23-25
Week 10..... Chapters 26-28
Week 11..... Chapters 29-30
Week 12..... Chapters 31-32
Week 13..... Conclusion

18 Week Reading Schedule

Week 1...... Chapters 1-2
Week 2...... Chapters 3-4
Week 3...... Chapters 5-6
Week 4...... Chapters 7-8
Week 5...... Chapter 9
Week 6...... Chapters 10-11
Week 7...... Chapter 12
Week 8...... Chapters 13-14
Week 9...... Chapters 15-16
Week 10..... Chapters 17-18
Week 11..... Chapters 19-20
Week 12..... Chapter 21
Week 13..... Chapter 22
Week 14..... Chapters 23-24
Week 15..... Chapters 25-26
Week 16..... Chapters 27-28
Week 17..... Chapters 29-30
Week 18..... Chapters 31-32

CHAPTER 1 – "WHAT GOOD DOES IT DO?"

Please note that all parenthetical notes refer to *A Praying Life* by Paul Miller.

1. Paul writes, "Kim's muteness was testimony to a silent God. Prayer, it seemed, doesn't work." When in your life has prayer not seemed to work? Tell your story (or stories) below (p. 14, first paragraph).

2. Paul writes of quiet cynicism, spiritual weariness and doubts that grow in us. Which of these do you relate most easily to? How do you see that (p. 14, second paragraph)?

3. Think about how you pray now. What is frustrating to you about prayer (pp. 14-15)?

4. Paul writes, "Praying exposes how self-preoccupied we are and uncovers our doubts. It was easier on our faith *not* to pray." Why is it easier on our faith *not* to pray? What does Paul mean by this (p. 15)?

5. What is it about American culture that makes it particularly difficult for you to pray (pp. 15-16)?

6. Imagine that prayer is like being on the phone with your earthly father. What is it like to talk with your heavenly Father?

a. Dry ("What do I say?")
b. Desperate ("I'm calling because I'm really in trouble and I don't know who else to call.")
c. Dutiful ("I'm calling because it's a special day or scheduled time.")
d. Drowsy ("I just can't keep my eyes open—gonna need some coffee...")
e. Disconnected ("Hello? Is anybody there?")
f. Distracted ("Uh, sorry, Dad, I gotta run...gotta get to work.")
g. Distant ("Do you even care what's going on with me?")
h. Dependent ("I can't make it through the day without talking to you.")
i. Delightful ("Can you believe we've been on the phone for a whole hour already?")
j. All of the above, at different times.

7. In Paul's story about Ashley's contact, what parts do you connect with? Recall an experience when God specifically answered a prayer (pp. 17-18).

CHAPTER 2 – WHERE WE ARE HEADED

1. How is prayer like having a good meal with friends (pp. 19-20)?

2. Read Revelation 3:20. What kind of God would describe prayer as a meal? What does this tell you about what Jesus is like?

3. What happens when we make prayer the center, our focus (p. 20)?

4. Describe the differences between an isolated prayer life and a prayer-intertwined life (p. 21).

5. After reading Paul's examples, what good things can come out of a prayer-intertwined life (p. 21, second paragraph)?

6. In what ways is learning to pray similar to growing up (p. 21)?

7. How is prayer a window into God's story for you (p. 22)?

8. How does prayer give birth to hope (pp. 22-23)?

9. How does a praying life affect a busy life (pp. 23-24)?

10. How does the prospect of having a vibrant, powerful praying life make you feel?

   a. Anxiety ("What if something—or nothing—happens?")
   b. Anticipation ("I can't wait—let's go!")
   c. Awe ("Who me, have that kind of relationship with God?")
   d. Apathy ("Who cares? It's not that important in my life.")
   e. Arrogance ("I don't need God's help—I can do life myself.")
   f. Alienation ("He probably won't listen to MY prayers.")
   g. A combination of more than one.

PART 1

LEARNING
TO PRAY
LIKE A
CHILD

CHAPTER 3 – BECOME LIKE A LITTLE CHILD

1. In what ways does Jesus want us to become like little children (pp. 29-32)?

2. Describe the differences between coming to God messy and coming put together—using the chart below (pp. 31-32).

	Coming Messy	Coming Put Together
What does it look like?		
How does God respond?		
What's hard about it?		

3. Why is it so important to come to God just as you are (pp. 32-34)? Why can this be so hard for us?

4. Read Mark 2:13-17. What kind of people did Jesus come for? What kind of person must Jesus have been like – that "tax collectors and sinners" enjoyed him?

5. How does the knowledge that you can come to this same Jesus, distracted, weary and cynical (like Nathaniel) impact you? How is this like the gospel?

6. What is the heart of prayer (pp. 34-35)?

7. Take time, right now, to come to God messy, for just five minutes. What was that experience like for you? Jot down a few words that come to mind.

CHAPTER 4 – LEARN TO TALK WITH YOUR FATHER

1. Think of a child you know. What do they ask for? How often? In what way?

2. In what ways are you similar to and different from that child as you talk to your Father?

3. How does Jesus show His approval for those who exhibit a childlike faith? Read Matthew 8:5-13; Luke 7:1-9; Matthew 15:21-28; Mark 7:24-30.

4. Read Luke 18:1-8, Jesus' story of why you should always pray and not give up. What is this widow like? How is she persistent? What obstacles would she have potentially faced as a widow?

5. What do little children believe about their parents that keeps them pestering? Do you believe this about your Father? What is it that you want to pester God about?

6. Take five minutes to talk with God, "to play." Talk to him about what your mind wanders to. What was that like for you?

CHAPTER 5 – SPENDING TIME WITH YOUR FATHER

1. Why did Jesus need to pray?

2. What does Paul mean when he says, "Jesus defines himself only in relationship with his heavenly Father" (p. 45, paragraph 3)? How would your life look differently if you did the same?

3. How does Jesus love the Father (p. 46)? How does the knowledge that the Father loves you with this same intensity of a "one-person focus" impact you?

4. Write down all you observe about how Jesus prayed (pp. 47-48).

5. On page 47, Paul writes, "You don't create intimacy; you make room for it." How is this true with all relationships? What happens when we don't create time?

6. What objection to prayer do you relate to most (p. 49)?

7. What are some suggestions in the book (p. 50) that might help you have a more focused prayer time with your Father? Try them tomorrow!

CHAPTER 6 – LEARNING TO BE HELPLESS

1. Read Psalm 142. This psalm was written by David when he was in the cave, hiding from Saul (1 Sam. 23-24). What is David's emotional state in this psalm? Have you ever been in a similar state?

2. What words or phrases in the psalm show us David's helpless state?

3. What words or phrases show us David's trust in God's ability and willingness to act on his behalf?

4. What makes becoming helpless so difficult for us?

5. Why is helplessness the key to a praying life (pp. 54-55)?

6. Paul writes, "Prayer mirrors the gospel" (p. 55). How so?

7. Read pages 56-59. Working through Paul's descriptions, contrast mature Christians with immature Christians using the chart below. How does this compare with how we typically view maturity?

	Mature Christians	Immature Christians
Their view of self		
Their view of sin		
How they relate to God		

8. Is this a new view of maturity for you? If so, how does it encourage you?

9. Where are you feeling helpless *right now*? Write down your thoughts. Talk with your Father about these things. Remember he likes messy.

CHAPTER 7 – CRYING "ABBA" — CONTINUOUSLY

1. Paul writes, "We don't need self-discipline to pray continuously; we just need to be poor in spirit" (p. 66). Read Matthew 5:3. What does it mean to be poor in spirit? Why does the kingdom of heaven belong to people who are poor in spirit?

2. Read Matthew 18:3-4. How are children poor in spirit? Why is it necessary to enter the kingdom of heaven like a child?

3. Read Luke 18:9-17. What would make it easier for "sinners" to enter the kingdom of heaven than the "righteous"? What makes it easier for the poor in spirit to repent?

4. Several different things keep us from being poor in spirit.

a. Read Matthew 19:23-24. For whom is it difficult to enter the kingdom of heaven? Why?

b. Read Matthew 23:4-14. How are the Pharisees the opposite of poor in spirit? How do they "shut the door of the kingdom of heaven" in people's faces?

5. Paul writes, "Interrupting, selling and boasting are just a few of the things that draw me into continuous prayer, into continual childlike dependence on my Father. Each of us has our own list. We can let it drive us into a praying life" (p. 64). What is on your list? What sinful tendencies can drive you into continuous prayer?

6. Think about a recent situation in which you felt poor in spirit. As you recall how you need(ed) help, cry out loud, practicing prayer the way Bartimaeus did. Practice using the Jesus prayer, "Lord Jesus Christ, Son of God, have mercy on me, a sinner."

CHAPTER 8 – BENDING YOUR HEART TO YOUR FATHER

1. Where are you experiencing anxiety? What is your natural response to this chaos?

2. How is anxiety a warped, unused, broken prayer link? Why doesn't it work (pp. 70-71)?

3. Paul writes, "Anxiety is unable to relax in the face of chaos; continuous prayer clings to the Father in the face of chaos" (p. 71). Why can't anxiety relax? What makes prayer a much better alternative?

4. Read Psalm 131. What connection does the Psalmist make between pride and going after things that are too great, too marvelous (also translated "difficult" or "complex")? In what ways can anxiety be a form of pride? How does the Psalmist call us back to sanity?

5. Read Matthew 10:29-31. Think about your answer to question 1. How does it change your outlook to know that your Father has *numbered* the hairs on your head?

PART 2

LEARNING
TO TRUST
AGAIN

CHAPTER 9 – UNDERSTANDING CYNICISM

1. What is cynicism? What does it feel like?

2. How does cynicism entice (pp. 78-79)?

3. Why is cynicism so dangerous? How does it subtly shape how you see God and reality?

4. What are some of the fruits of cynicism?

5. How is cynicism the opposite of a praying life?

6. Paul writes, "Cynicism begins, oddly enough, with too much of the wrong kind of faith, with naïve optimism or foolish confidence" (p. 80, first paragraph). How is naïve optimism different from faith?

7. Read Psalm 23. What is true about God in this psalm? What is true about people? How does this further differentiate faith from naïve optimism?

8. Paul writes, "Without the Good Shepherd, we are alone in a meaningless story" (p. 81). Read Psalm 23 again. How does the Shepherd bring meaning to David's story? If David's God is your shepherd now, how might he be bringing meaning to your story?

> ## CYNICISM HOMEWORK
> For one day, try to record every cynical thought that enters your mind. When you catch yourself, pray quietly, "Lord Jesus, save me from my cynicism. Give me eyes to see you."

CHAPTER 10 – FOLLOWING JESUS OUT OF CYNICISM

For this chapter, questions are organized around five cures Jesus offers for cynicism.

1. Be Warm but Wary

    a. What does it mean to be warm but wary (pp. 83-85)?

    b. Read Matthew 10:16-22, 26, 28, 31-32, 34. How does Jesus respond to evil with faith?

    c. When Jesus died, how did he keep "in tension wariness about evil with a robust confidence in the goodness of his Father" (p. 83)?

    d. How can we keep informed and vigilant without cultivating a cynical spirit?

2. Learn to Hope Again

a. Paul's friend said, "Expect nothing. Then if something good happens, be thankful." How can this attitude be compelling? How does it reflect cynicism? How does it kill hope and affect our prayers?

b. Why can we hope (pp. 85-86)?

c. Where do we learn how to hope? Where do we start?

3. Cultivate a Childlike Spirit

Paul writes on page 87, "Both the child and the cynic walk through the valley of the shadow of death. The cynic focuses on the darkness; the child focuses on the Shepherd." Read Psalm 23. How does focusing on the Shepherd lift the fog of cynicism?

4. Cultivating a Thankful Spirit

a. Paul writes, "Nothing undercuts cynicism more than a spirit of thankfulness. You begin to realize your whole life is a gift" (p. 89). How does thankfulness help us? How is it different from naïve optimism?

b. Think of a time when expressing gratitude to God dispelled bitterness or changed your perspective on a difficult situation. Describe what happened.

c. Read Psalm 23 again. Drift through your day yesterday. How was the Shepherd good to you? Thank God for his goodness to you.

5. Cultivating Repentance

a. How is cynicism two-faced (pp. 91-92)?

b. How does being cynical hinder us from cultivating repentance?

c. Paul writes, "Repentance brings the split personality together and thus restores integrity to the life" (p. 92). Read 1 Samuel 17:17-18, 26-29. What does this split personality look like in Eliab? How is David a contrast to this?

d. Have you recently been misjudged in your motive for doing or saying something? What do you learn from David's example? Or, have you cynically misjudged someone else, like Eliab? How were you two-faced? Repent of the specifics before God.

CHAPTER 11 – DEVELOPING AN EYE FOR JESUS

This chapter offers the last cure for cynicism: looking for Jesus.

1. Where do you look for Jesus (pp. 96-97)?

2. Practice looking for Jesus. Below write down where you see him.

3. How does looking for evidence of Jesus' presence cure our cynicism?

PART 3

LEARNING
TO ASK
YOUR
FATHER

CHAPTER 12 – WHY ASKING IS SO HARD

1. What is secularism (p. 105)?

2. Where does secularism relegate faith?

3. What does the Enlightenment do with prayer? How has this given birth to cynicism (pp. 106-108)?

4. On pages 108-110 we read the story of Dana Tierney, a writer for *The New York Times*, and her 4-year-old son Luke. In this story, who do you relate more with? Why?

5. From Dana's perspective, how do people with faith see the world?

6. How does the Enlightenment worldview rob us of childlike curiosity and wonder?

7. Think about this past week, focusing on your relationships with friends, neighbors, colleagues, and family. Were there ways this Enlightenment mindset colored your interactions, particularly when it came to faith? Were there situations in which you might have too easily dismissed faith or conversely been embarrassed by your faith?

8. What happens to us when we see the world as "my Father's world"? What is it like when we're filled with the "expansiveness of spirit" Dana refers to (p. 110)?

9. How does this mindset help us to pray about things like science experiments?

10. What are your "science experiments"? What areas of your life have you not yet considered praying about?

CHAPTER 13 – WHY WE CAN ASK

1. On page 113, Paul writes, "The issue of power – the ability to make a difference, to change something – is at the heart of asking." Why does power matter so much when it comes to asking?

2. Paul writes, "Learned desperation is at the heart of a praying life" (p. 114). Think about times you have been desperate. Did this change how you prayed? How so?

3. Read 2 Chronicles 6:14, 18-21. This is the prayer Solomon prays when he dedicates the temple he built for God. Find the words or phrases that point to an infinite God. Then, find the words or phrases that point to a personal God.

4. What is appealing to you about this infinite yet personal God? Why can you ask him?

5. Paul writes, "A praying life opens itself to an infinite, searching God. As we shall see, we can't do that without releasing control, without constantly surrendering our will to God. 'Your will be done, on earth as it is in heaven' is actually scary" (p. 117). What's scary about it?

CHAPTER 14 – HOW PERSONAL IS GOD?

1. Why does asking nothing of God seem spiritual? What's wrong with this?

2. How do the worldviews of Neoplatonism, the Enlightenment and Buddhism affect how we think about prayer?

3. Read Matthew 7:7-11. How is Jesus' worldview different from the ones above?

4. Read the section titled Pajamas and Milk (pp. 123-124). What strikes you about these stories?

5. Paul writes, "Prayer is a moment of incarnation—God with us. God involved in the details of my life" (p. 125). When have you seen God involved in the details of your own life? What was that like?

6. Why do we not like to ask (p. 125)?

7. Paul writes, "If you are going to enter this divine dance we call prayer, you have to surrender your desire to be in control....You've got to let God take the lead" (p. 128). What about your life do you want to control and not give to God? How do you think he's going to mess it up (pp. 130-131)?

8. Talk with God honestly about what you wrote above. Explain to him your fears.

CHAPTER 15 – WHAT DO WE DO WITH JESUS' EXTRAVAGANT PROMISES ABOUT PRAYER?

1. Read Jesus' promises in John 14:13-14, John 15:7, 16 and John 16:23-24. What about these promises makes you nervous? Have you ever asked God for anything and it didn't happen? How did that affect you?

2. What is correct about what the scholars say about Jesus' extravagant promises? What do they miss?

3. Read James 4:2-3, where James comes to the rescue. Then look at the chart on page 132.

   a. The first danger is the cliff of "Not Asking." What does James say about this? Does this describe your tendency in prayer? How so?

   b. The second danger is the cliff of "Asking Selfishly." What does James say about this? Does this describe your tendency in prayer? How so?

4. Read Mark 14:36. What two antidotes does Jesus offer to both these dangers in prayer? How does he avoid the "Not Asking" cliff? How does he avoid the "Asking Selfishly" cliff?

5. Look again at the verses from question 1. Why does Jesus tell us over and over to ask (pp. 134-135)? What is he concerned about?

6. What things do we tend not to ask God about? Make a list.

7. Reread John 14:13-14. What qualification is given to the promise, "Ask anything and I will do it"? What does it mean to pray in Jesus' name (p. 135)?

8. Reread John 15:7 and pages 138-139. What is one of the best ways to learn to abide? How does the fine print "if you abide in me, and my words abide in you" affect our asking?

9. What do you want God to do for you? Talk with him about what you write below. Remember, abiding can't begin to happen until the real you meets the real God.

CHAPTER 16 - WHAT WE DON'T ASK FOR: "OUR DAILY BREAD"

1. Paul writes, "Often our need for daily bread opens doors to deeper heart needs for real food" (p. 142). How have you seen this happen in your own life?

2. How does someone who is abiding pray differently from someone who is not abiding? Describe how the "asking" looks different. How does each respond to Jesus as King, as Lord? To the body of Christ (pp. 142-144)?

3. How does Paul distinguish between wisdom and guidance? Why does it seldom occur to us to ask God for advice and wisdom (p. 145)?

4. What do you learn from Paul's experience about asking for wisdom (pp. 145-147)?

5. Think of a situation in which you need wisdom. Write down the details, your questions, etc. What would it look like for you to ask God for wisdom with an abiding heart, a surrendered will? How would you involve the body of Christ?

CHAPTER 17 – WHAT WE DON'T ASK FOR: "YOUR KINGDOM COME"

1. What stages does God take the husband through as he begins to pray for his wife? How does he become the gospel for her (pp. 149-153)?

2. Think of someone you know who you want to see change in—but to ask for it feels either too controlling or hopeless. Write below one specific way that you'd like to see that person change.

3. How do you do the same thing described above?

4. Reverse your critical spirit. What are you thankful for about this person?

5. What makes it hard to pray for change in ourselves (p. 153)?

6. Paul writes, "The fatalism inherent in so much modern psychology immobilizes us." Think about the past week. Were there times in which you felt stuck, trapped by your feelings? If applicable, describe what happened (p. 153).

7. What does it mean that King Jesus brings the possibility of real change and hope to you (p. 154)?

8. What is one thing in our culture that bugs you? Talk to God about it; explain to him why it bothers you. Ask him to bring change.

CHAPTER 18 – SURRENDER COMPLETELY: "YOUR WILL BE DONE"

1. Paul unpacks an incident with Andrew (pp. 155-157). What did self-will look like in this situation? How might Paul have thought and acted if he'd been depending on Jesus?

2. Take a couple of days to read Matthew 5-7.

a. In chapter 5, how does Jesus close the door to self-will when it comes to relationships? What is he calling us to give up?

b. In chapter 6, how does Jesus challenge self-will? What does he call people to let go of?

c. What doors to self-will does Jesus close in chapter 7?

d. Of the different doors Jesus closes, which one "hurts" you the most?

3. How are prayer and self-will at odds? What is the fruit of each (pp. 160-161)?

4. As you think about your life, where are you resorting to self-will instead of prayer?

5. Paul writes, "Prayer is the positive side of the surrendered will" (p. 159). How is prayer an antidote to self-will? What can God do for us when we abide that he can't do for us when we're spinning our wheels in self-will?

6. Return to question 2d. Invite Jesus to close the door that "hurts" the most, admitting to him the silliness of insisting that door stay open.

PART 4

LIVING
IN YOUR
FATHER'S
STORY

CHAPTER 19 – WATCHING A STORY UNFOLD

1. How did Paul's prayers for Emily shape him (pp. 166-168)?

2. How did Paul love Emily better because he was praying?

3. How did God begin to answer Paul's prayers for Emily? How did his story for her begin to unfold?

4. What are some typical ways you try to change others?

5. So, how's that working for you?

6. In the middle of page 167, Paul writes, "Until you are convinced that you can't change your child's [or any person's] heart, you will not take prayer seriously." What does prayer do that all other methods can't do?

7. At some point, we give up our ability to change others. When this happens, what is the difference between giving up while on the road of Good Asking and giving up off the cliff of Despair (p. 170)?

8. Paul writes, "If a ship is off a few degrees, it is imperceptible at first, but over time it becomes a vast distance. I was praying to prevent the distance of a heart gone astray" (p. 166). Think about one of your kids, or someone close to you who you love as Paul loved Emily. What bend in his/her heart troubles or frazzles you? What can you pray for him/her in response to this?

CHAPTER 20 – A FATHER'S LOVE

1. What does it look like to pray in faith? What does it not look like (pp. 174, 177)?

2. What did God do for Emily through Paul's prayers? Make a list of all that he did.

3. How can staying on the road of Good Asking help us move toward the person for whom we are praying?

4. What hope can we have if we have known broken images of God in our fathers, bosses, pastors, or other leaders? How is this particularly meaningful to you?

CHAPTER 21 – UNANSWERED PRAYER: UNDERSTANDING THE PATTERNS OF STORY

1. Has it ever hurt you to hope? What happened that made/makes hope so hard?

2. What is your desert? Where is there a large gap between hope and reality in your life?

3. Paul gives three pictures of where we can go in the desert: denial, determination and despair. Which one best describes where you go (pp. 181-182)?

    a. If denial, what reality are you not facing?

    b. If determination, in what ways are you using your self-will to close the gap?

c. If despair, how have you partaken of the bread of bitterness (p. 184)?

4. Read Genesis 15:1-6; 16:1-6. Both Abram and Sarai live in the promise of God giving them a child and the reality of Sarai's barren womb. How do they respond to this desert? In what ways are you like them in your desert?

5. What does God do for people in the desert (pp. 184-185)?

CHAPTER 22 – HOW GOD PLACES HIMSELF IN THE STORY

1. Read Matthew 15:21-28. How does Jesus enter the Canaanite woman's story? What does he do for her (pp. 189-191)?

2. Generally speaking, where is God in our stories? Why is he not a magic prayer machine (p. 192)?

3. Read John 20:11-18. Why does Jesus hold back with Mary (pp. 192-193)?

4. Paul writes, "When we suffer, we long for God to speak clearly, to tell us the end of the story and, most of all, to show himself. But if he showed himself fully and immediately, if he answered all the questions, we'd never grow; we'd never emerge from our chrysalis because we'd be forever dependent" (p. 194). Look at the Scriptures below to discover what God grows in us through waiting.

　　a. Read Hebrews 11:1. What is faith? What makes the desert a greenhouse for faith?

b. Read Romans 8:23-24. Why can hope only grow when we can't see?

c. Read Isaiah 40:31. What happens to those who wait upon the Lord?

d. Read 2 Corinthians 5:7. How do we walk?

e. Read 2 Corinthians 4:17-18. What are our temporary, light afflictions producing for us? What do they help us look at?

5. As you think about your own desert, how do you see/have you seen God lingering at the edge? In what ways do/did you perceive him growing faith in you?

CHAPTER 23 – PRAYING WITHOUT A STORY

1. On page 198, Paul outlines two approaches to a praying life—one believes there is no story, while the other lives in the story God is weaving. As you look at the fruits of each category, which fruits do you see manifested in your life?

2. Paul differentiates between "making an isolated prayer request and praying in the context of the story that God is weaving" (p. 201). What does he mean by this?

3. What three things do we need to keep in mind as we live in our Father's story? Of these three, which is most challenging for you (p. 201)?

4. In what ways has it been challenging for you to stay in God's story?

5. Paul writes, "Be on the lookout for strange gifts. God loves to surprise us with babies in swaddling clothes lying in mangers" (p. 201). Has God surprised you with strange gifts in your desert? What did he give?

6. How is God an artist in how he tells stories? How do you see his craftsmanship in the story he is writing for you? What patterns/ themes are emerging? How is he developing your character (pp. 202-203)?

Chapter 24 – Hope: The End of the Story

1. Why can we hope when we pray (pp. 205-206)? Why can we dream big?

2. In what way could simply focusing on knowing God resemble another version of the despair chart (see page 183)?

3. Read Matthew 7:7-11. Paul writes, "I have prayed for humility, and it dawned on me that God was answering my prayer. I would have preferred humility to come over me like magic. Instead, God teaches humility in humble places. He keeps me sane by letting me pick up dog manure after I've spoken at a conference. What I thought was a stone was really a loaf of bread" (p. 208). Have you ever thought that God had given you a stone (bad gift), but it turned out to be a loaf of bread (good gift)? What happened?

4. Do you believe that your Father "will pick you up, carry you out into the night, and make your life sparkle" (p. 210)? Are you willing to be enchanted?

5. How is this willingness to be enchanted different from denial or naïve optimism?

6. Read Ephesians 3:20. According to this verse, what can God do?

7. Reflect a little on the chart on page 209. Paul writes, "As we wait and pray, God weaves his story and creates a wonder....We are learning to watch for the story to unfold, to wait for the wonder" (p. 209). How does it affect you that God wants to bring your story together in such a way that fills you with wonder?

8. Dream big before God right now. Record your dreams below.

CHAPTER 25 – LIVING IN GOSPEL STORIES

1. Paul writes, "The gospel, the Father's gift of his Son to die in our place, is so breathtaking that since Jesus' death, no one has been able to tell a better story. If you want to tell a really good story, you have to tell a gospel story" (p. 213). What are the key themes in the gospel story?

2. How does God retell these themes in your own life?

3. How are we blessed when we live in a gospel story (bottom of page 214-215)?

4. How does a gospel story give meaning to suffering?

5. How does living in a gospel story make us more authentic people? How do we become people of integrity?

PART 5

PRAYING IN REAL LIFE

CHAPTER 26 – USING PRAYER TOOLS

1. Are you someone who likes systems, or doesn't? If not, why not?

2. If you do like systems, how do you keep track of important dates or what you need to accomplish?

3. What are some of the benefits of having a system for dates or tasks?

4. What might some of the benefits be for writing down our prayer requests?

5. According to Paul, why do we need a prayer system (pp. 222-223)?

6. In what ways should we be careful about systems (pp. 223-224)?

CHAPTER 27 – KEEPING TRACK OF
THE STORY:
USING PRAYER CARDS

1. In what ways might prayer cards be more helpful than a list?

2. Paul talks about using Scripture to shape his prayers for people (p. 225). Read the following Scriptures, noting the phrases used to describe what the Word of God is or what the Word of God does. Which ones give you confidence in the effectiveness of using God's Word in prayer?

   a. Psalm 119:105

   b. Isaiah 55:10-11

   c. Romans 10:17

   d. Ephesians 6:17-18

e. 2 Timothy 3:16-17

f. Hebrews 4:12

g. 1 Peter 1:22-25

3. Take time this week to build a small deck of prayer cards, picking Scripture for each person you pray for and 1-2 ways you want to see God bring change. Begin to use these cards.

4. What was it like? Helpful? Unhelpful?

CHAPTER 28 – PRAYER WORK

1. Read Mark 4:26-29 and pages 236-237.

   a. The farmer plants first. Isn't this the opposite of what we do? Paul writes, "[It] seldom occurs to us to plant the seed of thoughtful praying because we think people like _____ don't change" (p. 237). Think of a recent situation in which you haven't thoughtfully prayed, but rushed into action. Describe what happened.

   b. The farmer then waits, which is another thing we don't do well. Paul writes, "Second, if we do pray, we don't watch and wait. We want the answer now. We grumble right at the point when God is about to do his biggest work" (p. 237). Have you ever gotten impatient and "uncovered" a prayer seed which you had planted, only to stunt or destroy its growth? Describe what happened.

   c. At last the farmer harvests. Paul writes, "Finally, we don't recognize the harvest when it comes....we forget that Jesus' image of reaping is hard work....Instead of working in partnership with God, we attack the problem" (p. 237). When have you missed the harvest because you were too busy attacking the problem?

2. What happens when we do "prayer work" backwards? What is frequently going on when we say, "Prayer doesn't work"?

3. How did God answer Paul's prayer for Bob? How did God involve Paul in answering this prayer?

4. How might God be involving you in answering your prayers?

CHAPTER 29 – LISTENING TO GOD

1. "I don't want you to have any goals this year. I'm going to work on your character" (p. 239). When Paul heard these words, how did he know it was God's voice (pp. 241-242)?

2. What do we miss when we focus on "Word Only"?

3. Read Ephesians 6:17-18. How are the Spirit and the Word of God connected?

4. What happens when we divorce the Word of God from his Spirit (pp. 242-243, 246)?

5. What do we miss and confuse when we focus on "Spirit Only"? How is this dangerous (pp. 243-246)?

6. Read John 14:16-17, 26 and John 16:7-8, 13-14. Jot down all the phrases that describe who the Spirit is or what the Spirit does. Why do we need the Word of God and the Spirit when we pray?

7. How do you cultivate a listening heart? Why can't you learn to listen while living a life that is not in surrender to God (p. 247)?

8. What's the problem with focusing on "listening"?

9. What happens to David and God's thoughts, as David is obedient (p. 248)?

CHAPTER 30 – PRAYER JOURNALING: BECOME AWARE OF THE INTERIOR JOURNEY

1. How does journaling help us to see the story God is writing for us (pp. 250-251)?

2. How is the spiritual pilgrimage different from the quest for self-fulfillment (p. 252)?

3. Paul writes on page 254, "Writing in a prayer journal helps us to articulate the state of our hearts." How does journaling help Paul discover the state of his heart?

4. If you don't regularly journal, give prayer journaling a try for a week. Get a journal, and be honest with God in it about where you are. Then let Scripture speak to your heart, and respond back to him in writing. At the end of the week read over your entries. Do you see any patterns emerge? Convictions?

5. If you do regularly journal, what do you learn from this chapter that you could apply to journaling?

CHAPTER 31 – REAL-LIFE PRAYING

1. Contrast hunting for an experience with God with inviting God into your life experience.

2. What do you appreciate about Paul's real-life praying? What about it particularly encourages you?

3. How does Paul deal with interruptions? What do you learn from this?

4. If someone were to walk into your real-life praying, how would they describe it?

90

CHAPTER 32 – UNFINISHED STORIES

1. Paul discusses the Babylon captivity. Read Psalm 137:1-6. What was the perspective of the Jewish people while in captivity?

2. Read Haggai 2:1-3. What were the Jewish people thinking when they returned from captivity and rebuilt the temple? Read Haggai 2:6-9. What was the future hope God proclaimed to them?

3. In your own words, list what God did for Israel through their unfinished story, their captivity. Which of these things might God be doing for you in your "captivity", your unfinished story?

4. As he did for Israel, God is weaving for you a story so rich, so fragrant of him that you cannot imagine how good it is. Read 1 Corinthians 2:9 and bask in its truth. What does this mean for you?

LEADER'S GUIDE

LEADER'S GUIDE FOR 13 WEEK SCHEDULE

How to Prepare

- Read chapters ahead of time. As you read, highlight or underline a couple of things that were especially helpful or meaningful to you.
- Work through the discussion questions.
- Familiarize yourself with the questions from the leader notes. All questions you're to ask are in **bold type**. Find a way to easily reference these questions while leading.
- We recommend you purchase a flip chart, because it allows you to review previous lessons. This ✐ symbol in the guide indicates what you are to write on your chart. Whenever possible, write out charts and questions beforehand.
- Plan on each study taking about 70 minutes. This includes prayer.

How to Lead

Leading a study in prayer is an adventure, led by the Spirit. As a leader, what matters most is loving people in your group and bringing them to Jesus. This study guide is meant to be a tool to that end, but not the end in itself. As you lead, take time to listen to people, to enjoy them. Resist the temptation to rush ahead, finish people's sentences, or fill uncomfortable silences. At the same time, you want to avoid discussions that wander off topic. Gently return your group to the questions, saying, "That's interesting, but would you mind if we talked about that later? Let's move on to..." As you lead with an ear to the Spirit's convicting and comforting, you will discover the beautiful stories God is weaving in people's lives. What a privilege!

The best way to keep in tune with these stories is through prayer. At the end of each study, even if you have to cut your discussion short, devote fifteen minutes to prayer—practicing what you learned. During this time you may want to have people pair up to foster more intimacy, or stay together. This is up to you. (If your group is mixed gender, we encourage you to split up according to the same gender.) At the end of each discussion section are suggestions for prayer. We do not mean for each of these suggestions to be followed, but for you to pick one or two suggestions that are best for your group. For instance, in Week 6, people in your group discussion may have been struck by praying for a specific change in our culture. Rather than read each of the prayer suggestions, invite people to focus on praying for our culture. You're just following the Spirit's lead. If it's not clear what you should do, give people a couple of choices.

When you pray, we recommend that you set in place guidelines, and post them where they are visible.

Including Newcomers to Prayer

So many people are hungry for God. When Jesus tells the story of the Pharisee and the tax collector praying, it's the tax collector's prayer that the Father hears. Ironically, when it comes to bringing our friends to Jesus, sometimes our prayers get in the way. The longer we pray, the more spiritual we sound. The more we can intimidate. Then, without realizing it, we miss the short quieter prayers of our friends, "God help me! I'm a mess!" It isn't complicated leading people to Jesus. It's just a matter of creating space where we pray more simply, and allow our real selves to meet our real Father.

We welcome your feedback. Please email us at info@seeJesus.net.

WEEK 1

Introduction (10 min)

Welcome people to your group and explain the following:
- **Read chapters ahead of time. As you read, note passages that were especially helpful or meaningful to you.**
- **Work through the discussion questions from this schedule.**
- **Each week, we'll set aside time to pray.** Explain the below guidelines.

Prayer Guidelines

Our intent behind these guidelines is simply that they be helpful in directing you to pray. You may want to make your own or modify what we have. Whatever you do, we recommend you type it up, and put it somewhere visible where people can see it each week:
- No gossip. Sadly, we can be notorious for disguising our gossip through prayer requests. But let it not be.
- Limit your prayer to what you can say in a breath. This way our prayers will feel more like conversation and less like monologues.

Chapter 1 (30 min)

1. Start by asking participants, **"What are your frustrations with prayer?"** Invite people to be candid; this is not the time for Sunday school answers! ✍ Write everyone's answer on the flip chart.
2. Follow this up by discussing questions 2 and 6. Being vulnerable yourself will help others to be vulnerable.
3. Read "Ashley's Contact" (pp. 17-18).
4. Invite people, **"Talk about a time when God specifically answered a prayer. What happened?"**

Chapter 2 (30 min)

1. Ask, **"Which aspect of 'the praying life' spoke to you most? Why?"** Encourage people to be brief – you just want to get a sense of what impacted them.

2. Explain, **"We'll get to unpack some aspects of a praying life this evening, but probably not all. Let's look at the first aspect. How is prayer like having a meal with good friends?"**

3. Follow this up, reading the last two paragraphs from page 20. Ask, **"What happens when we make prayer our focus?"**

4. Continue reading from page 21, the fourth paragraph: "You don't experience God; you get to know Him. You submit to Him. You enjoy Him. He is, after all, a person." Refer back to question 6 from chapter 1 and ask, **"What does it mean that God is a person? Let's go back to our phone call with a person—God. Why might our view of God's personhood affect our conversation with him? Which of the experiences in our prayer might be different if we view God as a person?"**

5. End by discussing questions 9 and 10.

Prayer Suggestion (10 min)

Thank God for one aspect of a praying life from chapter 2.

WEEK 2

Introduction

Ask, **"What are some words that describe children—how they behave, talk, play, look?"**

Chapter 3 (20 min)

1. Lead people through questions 1-2. When you get to 2, ✍ write the "Coming Messy" chart (found on p. 19 of this guide) on your flip chart, and fill it in with people's own observations, using their words.

2. Sit on questions 3, 4, and 5. These are the heart of this chapter, and in fact, the very heart of prayer. How we come to God mirrors the gospel. People must understand that God wants them to come messy. This is the good news of the gospel. He will have us no other way!

Chapter 4 (20 min)

1. Jump into questions 1-2, further filling out what it means to come as a child to God.

2. In question 4, you want to leave people with a strong impression of what this widow was like, and the obstacles she faced. The more people think about her obstacles, the more they will be able to transition to thinking about their own pestering (question 5).

3. Discuss question 5.

4. At the end, describe how "playing" and "coming to God messy" are two sides of the same coin — coming to God as you are.

Chapter 5 (20 min)

1. Read the first paragraph on page 43. Ask, **"Why did Jesus need to pray?"**

2. Discuss question 2. Understanding this will lay the foundation for the rest of the chapter.

3. Read together John 5:1-6. Ask, **"What do you observe about how Jesus focuses on this man? How can you tell that he is focused on him?"** ✍ Write down people's answers.

4. Immediately follow this up, and ask, **"How does it affect you that the Father loves you with the same one-on-one attention when you pray?"**

5. For question 4, ✍ record everything your group observes about how Jesus prayed.

6. Then, ask question 5, helping people to grasp what happens when we don't invest in relationships.

7. If you are meeting in a larger group, have people break up in groups of two to three. If your group is small, just stay together. Have people share their reflections on questions 6-7, and invite each person to pick a suggestion to try the following week.

Prayer Suggestions (15 min)
Choose from one of the following:
- Practice coming to God messy and/or playing.
- Pester God in a childlike way.

WEEK 3

Introduction
Ask, **"In John 15, Jesus said, 'Apart from me you can do nothing.' In other words, apart from him, we are helpless to do life in a way that is pleasing to God. But being helpless is hard. Why does helplessness make us feel uneasy?"**

Chapter 6 (30 min)

1. Read together Psalm 142, explaining that this psalm was written by David when he was in the cave (I Sam. 23-24), escaping King Saul's murderous intent toward him. Unpack your answers to questions 1-4, sticking to the Psalm as much as possible for your answers.

2. Invite people to share a situation in which they were helpless to act on their own and had to rely on others. These questions lay the groundwork for working through the central questions of this chapter: 5-7.

3. For questions 5-6, ✍ write people's answers on the flip chart.

4. For question 7, ✍ write out the chart from page 57 on your flip chart and fill it in.

5. Conclude your discussion with questions 8-9. People may feel more free to answer question 9 if you lead in being vulnerable. No one likes to admit helplessness!

Chapter 7 (20 min)

1. Using your flip chart, ✍ write "What is poor in spirit?" across the top. Ask people questions 1 and 2, recording their answers on the chart.

2. Read aloud from Mark 10:46-52 and Luke 18:9-17. Ask, **"What makes blind Bartimaeus and the tax collector poor in spirit?"** ✍ Add their answers to the chart.

3. Ask, **"When Jesus tells the story of the tax collector and Pharisee, what connection does he make between the poor-in-spirit and repentance?"**

4. Ask question 5, inviting people to share personally.

Chapter 8 (25 min)

1. Explain, **"In this session we'll be looking at the first of two things that can paralyze us in prayer: worry."** Discuss people's responses to the first question, by just highlighting the second portion. There will be a time later when people can talk about their anxieties more in depth when they pray.

2. Ask, **"Think of a situation right now where you are experiencing anxiety. What is your natural response to this?"**

3. Jump into questions 2 and 3, filling out how anxiety is warped, and how prayer is so much better.

4. Read together Psalm 131, and together respond to question 4.

5. Ask, **"Does this mean we shouldn't go after complex things? How might it be possible to go after complex things with a child-like heart?"**

6. Ask: **"How can you check your heart? What are the warning signs of it becoming prideful?"** Hint: what is this chapter about?

Prayer Suggestions (15 min)

Pray like Bartimaeus and the tax collector – if possible go into separate rooms in case you want to get noisy. You can:

• Pray about your list of sinful tendencies that can drive you to pray continually. Repent of these poor-in-spirit style. Then, ask God to use these patterns to make you more like Bartimaeus.

• Explain to God your anxieties. Ask him to help you, remembering that he is God and you are not.

WEEK 4

Introduction

Ask, "Have you ever felt like you're on a rough stretch of road with no end in sight, or like you've been let down just once too often? Last week we learned to call out in childlike trust to our Abba Father when we are feeling weak or helpless. This week we'll look at the alternative: to become defeated or cynical."

Chapter 9 (30 min)

1. Explain, "**Before we see cynicism's effects, we need to see what it is.**" Jump into questions 1-3, helping people to describe cynicism and how it tempts, subtly corrupting.

2. For questions 4 and 5, draw the following chart on the flip chart. ✍ Write people's responses to questions 4 and 5 in the first "Fruit" row. For the next row ask, "**What drives us to cynicism?**"[naïve optimism] "**What core beliefs are at the center of naïve optimism?**" ✍ Record people's thoughts. Then ask, "**What drives us to a praying life?**" [faith, or the need for faith]

	Cynicism	A praying life
Fruit		
What drives us to:		
Core beliefs about God & people:		

3. Explain, "**Let's look at Psalm 23 to understand the core beliefs that are the center of faith. What is true about people in this psalm? What is true about God?**" ✍ Record observations on the above chart.

4. Ask, "**How is faith different from naïve optimism?**"

5. Continue with question 8. The more you help your group observe how God brought meaning to David's story, the more easily they will see God bringing meaning to their own stories. ✍ To help people grasp this, draw the following chart. Record people's answers in the corresponding spaces.

	David	You
How God brings meaning to:	{Say, "**Let's list what God does in Psalm 23.**"}	{Ask, "**How do you see God bringing meaning to your story as he did for David?**"}

100

Chapter 10 (25 min)

1. Ask the group, **"Which of Jesus' first four cures grabbed you – being warm but wary, learning to hope, becoming like a child, or having a thankful spirit?"**

2. Discuss the two most popular cures, based on their responses.

3. Lead the group on to cure five, "Cultivating Repentance," discussing the questions in this section.

Chapter 11 (15 min)

1. Based on questions 1 and 2, ask, **"What evidence of Jesus' presence have you seen recently?"** Come prepared with your own story to share.

2. Ask question 3.

Prayer Suggestions (15 min)

Choose one of the following:

• Pray together aloud, naming the ways in which you are two-faced. Ask God to change you.

• Read through Psalm 23, and thank God for how he is good to you, for how you have recently seen the presence of Jesus.

Cynicism Homework (5 min)

Read the homework assignment on page 36, and pass out a piece of paper to each person for recording. Explain that you will debrief this next week.

WEEK 5

Introduction

Teach, **"Last week we looked long and hard at cynicism and how to follow Jesus out of it through cautious optimism and a childlike, hopeful, grateful and repentant spirit that looks for evidence of His presence and power."** Ask, **"What did you learn about yourself through the cynicism exercise? What did you learn about cynicism? When you asked to see more of Jesus, what happened? How did that help?"**

Chapter 12 (20 min)

1. Begin by pointing to the diagram on page 105, explaining how secularism sees the world.

2. Ask questions 2 and 3.

3. Briefly summarize the story of Dana and her son Luke (pp. 108-110).

4. Ask question 4.

5. Read from the first paragraph on page 110, and ask questions 5-6.

6. As you discuss question 7, be prepared to share your own situation.

7. After a few minutes of sharing, recap the problem of a secular worldview — the false dichotomy that it sets up.

8. Ask questions 8 and 9.

9. As you ask question 10, help people to be as concrete as possible. ✍ Write people's answers on the flip chart.

Chapter 13 (15 min)

1. Ask question 1.

2. Have someone read aloud 2 Chronicles 6:14, 18-21. Explain the context of the passage.

3. On your flip chart ✍ draw the following chart. Fill in the chart with people's observations from the passage.

Infinite	Personal

4. Ask question 4. If time permits, ask question 5.

Chapter 14 (25 min)

1. Explain, **"Let's talk frankly about what we perceive as spiritual and unspiritual requests. Give me some candid examples."** Using the flip chart, ✍ write out the people's responses. Then ask question 1.

Spiritual Requests	Unspiritual Requests

2. Ask question 2, filling out the "why" behind this false dichotomy.

3. Ask question 3. Have someone read aloud from Matthew 7:7-11.

4. Work through questions 4-5. Read aloud from pp. 123-124.

5. Discuss question 6, citing the 2nd and 3rd paragraph on page 125.

6. Conclude with question 7.

Prayer Suggestions (15 min)

Invite people to split up into pairs and do one suggestion of the following:

• What details would you like to ask God about that you hadn't considered before? What are your pajamas and spilled milk? Ask God to provide for your needs, explaining to him the details.

• What areas of your life do you want to control rather than give to God? How do you think he might mess it up? Be honest with God, explaining your hang-ups, and ask him to change you, to help you trust him.

WEEK 6

Introduction

Teach, **"Last week we talked about this radical concept of an infinite-personal God. Before Christ, most cultures other than the Jews believed in tribal gods who were limited and distant, not infinite and personal. The Jews believed that the infinite God of the universe was concerned about individuals—unheard of! And the idea of the incarnation, the infinite God with us, was completely radical! They believed, as we do, that God interacts with history. But even though we say we believe this, prayer is still hard for us. In today's lesson, we get to ask ourselves if we really believe that the extravagant promises of Jesus about prayer are real. What do they mean? What are the implications? And how does that affect our praying life?"**

Chapter 15 (15 min)

1. Work through question 1, reading the verses aloud, and ✍ writing down what makes people nervous.
2. Move quickly through question 2, then read James 4:2-3.
3. Review the path of "Good Asking" illustrated on page 132. Ask, **"What is dangerous about each side?"**
4. Ask, **"Which side do you tend towards?"**
5. Discuss Jesus' two antidotes to wrong asking in question 4.
6. Ask question 5, encouraging people to become askers.
7. Write ✍ a list of what we don't ask for (question 6).
8. Discuss questions 7 and 8.

Chapter 16 (20 min)

1. Ask question 1, but don't spend too much time here. The idea is to remind people of last week's lesson—that it is good to ask.
2. Lead the group into question 2, ✍ drawing the following chart and filling it in with people's observations.

	Abiding Person	Not Abiding Person
How do they respond to Jesus as King?		
How do they ask God for help?		
How do they involve the body of Christ in their lives?		

It is important that people grasp what happens when we isolate praying from the rule of Jesus, from the body of Christ (his church). Even more significantly, we want people to understand what abiding looks like as we pray and interact with the body of Christ.

3. Flesh out questions 3 and 4.

4. Invite people to reflect on question 5 together. You'll likely only have time to listen to two people share. As people share, avoid the temptation to give advice. Instead, pray either now or at the end of your time.

Chapter 17 (30 min)

1. Discuss question 1.

2. Skip question 2. But before asking questions 3 and 4, say, **"Now keep this person in mind from question 2, but for confidentiality, don't say who they are when answering these next questions."**

3. Discuss questions 5-7.

4. If you have time, talk together about one thing in our culture that you want to see God change. What do you want God to do? ✍ Make a list together.

Prayer Suggestions (15 min)

Choose one of the following for your group.

• Think of a situation in which you need wisdom. Write down the details, your questions, etc. What would it look like for you to ask God for wisdom with an abiding heart? How would you ask? Would you surrender your will? How would you involve the body of Christ?

• Privately, think of a person you would like to see change. On your own, pray for change to come. Then ask God to show you how you might be sinning like him or her. Close by giving thanks for that person.

• Pray for change to come in one particular way in our larger culture.

WEEK 7

Introduction

Teach, **"Paul writes, 'At the center of self-will is me, carving a world in my image. At the center of prayer is God, carving me in his Son's image' (p. 156). This week we'll be looking at how our self-will stands in opposition to prayer, and how God can change us to pray with faith for others."**

Chapter 18 (35 min)

1. Discuss question 1 to get a sense of what self-will can look like.

2. Move on to question 2. On your flip chart, ✍ write, "Doors Jesus closes to self-will." Draw a copy of the chart on page 159.

3. Read Matthew 5:21-26, 27-30, 38-48. Say, **"Let's name all the doors Jesus closes here."** Next ask, **"What does he call us to give up when it comes to relationships?"**

4. Go on, reading Matthew 6:1-8, 16-34. Ask, **"Which doors does Jesus close to self-will in this passage? What is he asking us to give up?"**

5. Read Matthew 7:1-7. Ask again, **"Which doors does Jesus close to self-will in this passage? What is he asking us to give up?"**

6. Ask question 2.d.

7. Move into questions 3-5. Question 6 will be a prayer suggestion.

Chapter 19 (15 min)

1. Reflect together on questions 1-3, giving people a sense of the stories God unfolds when we pray.

2. Go into questions 4 and 5, looking at how our methods of changing others fall short.

3. For question 6, ✍ write on the flip chart, "What prayer does that other methods can't" and record people's observations.

4. Conclude with question 7. Question 8 will be a prayer suggestion.

Chapter 20 (15 min)

1. Summarize the Guatemala story from pages 173-177.

2. Ask questions 2 and 3, ✍ recording responses on your flip chart.

3. Wrap up with question 4.

4. Optional: consider asking someone in your group to share about how God has shown his love for them in spite of difficult role models.

Prayer Suggestions (15 min)

Choose one of the following suggestions to pray through:

- Go back to the door that "hurts" the most to close (from Chapter 18). This is the door Jesus wants to close. Invite Jesus to do that, admitting to him the silliness of insisting that this door stay open. Then invite Jesus to open the door to prayer.

- Reflect on the story God is telling in someone you love. How are you coming alongside of God and the story he's telling? Are there ways you are getting in the way? Pray to him, asking for insight into this.

- Paul writes, "If a ship is off a few degrees, it is imperceptible at first, but over time it becomes a vast distance. I was praying to prevent the distance of a heart gone astray" (p. 166). Think about one of your kids or someone else close to you, who you love as Paul loved Emily. What bend in his/her heart troubles you, frazzles you? What can you pray for him/her in response to this? Privately pray for this.

WEEK 8

Introduction

Teach, **"We've been talking about how God reveals the story he is telling in our lives. But what if, like Paul and Jill, we don't like our story? Yes, we can see that God is doing something; we just don't like what he's doing. We want to change a few chapters, rewrite the events, give it more—or less—drama, even delete some parts altogether. This week we'll be talking about life in the 'desert'—this place of pain, disappointment and lack of our own resources. We'll be asking, 'Where is God in this place? What is he up to?'"**

Chapter 21 (25 min)

1. Say, **"Turn to page 181 in *A Praying Life*. Take a couple of minutes to think about your desert."**
2. Ask question 2, using the questions to gently press into people's particular deserts.
3. Roughly ✍ sketch (you may want to do this beforehand) Paul's desert charts of despair, denial and determination (pp. 181-183). Discuss question 3, encouraging people to elaborate on specifics.
4. Read Genesis 15:1-6 and 16:1-6 and work through question 4.
5. Brainstorm all the good things God does in the desert – that he can't do anywhere else. ✍ Write people's ideas on the flip chart.

Chapter 22 (20 min)

1. Say, **"Let's first look at how God lingers at the edge,"** and discuss questions 1-3.
2. For question 4, have people read the Scriptures and answer the corresponding questions.
3. Afterwards, ask, **"So what does God grow in us through waiting?"** ✍ Record people's answers on the flip chart.
4. Discuss question 5.

Prayer Suggestions (15 min)

Choose one of the following:

- Are you in the desert right now? Share (as you feel comfortable) and let the group pray with you.
- Reflect on how God has grown you in the desert by lingering at the edge. Savor Psalm 63 and thank him for loving your soul more than life.

WEEK 9

Introduction

Teach, **"This week we're going to focus on how the story God is telling is so much bigger than anything we can imagine. To see this, we need to remember THE story God tells, the gospel story."**

Chapter 23 (15 min)

1. Begin with question 1, helping people flesh out the fruits they see in their lives.

2. Help participants to think positively by asking, **"How would you be different if you really believed you were living in your Father's story?"**

3. Ask questions 2 and 3.

4. Ask question 4. This focuses on what is most challenging for many, *actually* staying in the story, continuing to be engaged. Ask, **"How are you tempted to disengage from the story?"**

5. Question 5 is great for encouraging people who are struggling to stay in the story.

6. Finish with question 6.

Chapter 24 (20 min)

1. Discuss question 1, encouraging people that they can dream big because God is big.

2. Ask question 3, helping people to see what can seem like a stone might really bread. Ask, **"Are there areas in your life where you have dreamed big before God, but feel you have a stone?"**

3. Ask questions 4-7. As you reflect on these, help people to feel a sense of the wonder, the real wonder they will experience when they see God bring their story together.

Chapter 25 (20 min)

1. Discuss question 1. ✍ Write down people's answers, highlighting the key themes. This exercise will help them answer question 2 more easily.

2. Ask question 2.

3. For question 3, ✍ list all the blessings.

4. Ask question 4. Invite people to think of specific times when God has brought meaning to suffering through working out his gospel story in their lives. ✍ Record what God did.

5. Discuss the first part of question 5, helping people see that living in the gospel story (1) anchors us to our real source of love, the Father, and (2) helps us to live connected to our world while in sync with our Father's world.

6. Discuss the second part of question 5, "How do we become people of integrity?" After letting people talk, direct them to the bottom of page 214, and the top of 215, helping them see how repentance creates integrity.

Prayer Suggestions (15 min)
Choose one of the following:
- Think through the list of three things (p. 201) that help us live in our Father's story: 1) Don't demand the story go your way. 2) Look for the Storyteller. 3) Stay in the story. Which of these challenges you the most? Pray for one another accordingly.
- How do you see God's craftsmanship in the story he is writing for you? What patterns/themes are emerging? How is he developing your character? Take time to reflect and thank him for what he reveals to you.
- Take turns dreaming big before God. After each person dreams, pray with him or her for those dreams.
- Praise God for ways in which your life resembles the gospel story.

WEEK 10

Introduction
Teach, **"This week we'll be looking at several tools we can use to help us pray. To use Paul's metaphor – we're all disabled and need help. We'll first look at why tools can be helpful, and then move into a couple of specific tools to try: prayer cards and Scripture."**

Chapter 26 (15 min)
1. Lead with questions 1-2. For question 2, ✐ record people's answers on your flip chart.
2. Move quickly into questions 4-6, giving people a sense of why systems can be helpful and what pitfalls to avoid.

Chapter 27 (25 min)
1. Before you meet, ✐ write the verse references in question 2 on a flip chart. Leave room between them for responses.
2. Discuss question 1.
3. For question 2, assign each group member a verse to read. After each person reads, ask – **"What phrases are used to describe what the Word of God is or what the Word of God does?"** ✐ Write their answers on your chart.
4. After hearing all the answers, point to the chart and ask, **"Which ones give you confidence in the effectiveness of using God's Word in prayer?"**

5. Finish by debriefing prayer cards by asking questions 3 and 4. Affirm that this may work for some people, but not others. The point is to experiment in order to find the tools that work for you.

Chapter 28 (20 min)

1. Read together Mark 4:26-29. Sketch the following chart, leaving only the column titles and numbers. Invite people to compare and contrast the farmer with how we pray. Ask, **"What does the farmer do first, second and third? What do we do?"** As people answer, fill in the chart.

2. After people share their thoughts, explain how the farmer is just the opposite of us: we first WORK, then WATCH things fall apart, and then ASK when we give up. He first ASKS, then WATCHES God weave the story, and then WORKS alongside God.

How We Usually Pray	How the Farmer Works
1. We attack the problem [WORK]	1. He plants the seed of thoughtful praying. [ASK]
2. We watch things fall apart. [WATCH]	2. He watches and waits, looks for God's story. [WATCH]
3. Resort to prayer last minute. Frustrated, miss the story. [ASK]	3. Recognizes the harvest; works in partnership with God. [WORK]

3. Ask question 2.
4. Conclude by discussing questions 3-4.

Prayer Suggestions (15 min)

Choose one of the following for your group:

• Make a prayer card. Think of a situation or someone you'd like to pray for, and find Scripture you'd like to use in praying. Feel free to use the examples on pages 227-231 in *A Praying Life*.

• Think of a recent time when you approached a problem in the usual way. Now think about the farmer and retrace your steps, planting a seed of thoughtful prayer.

WEEK 11

Introduction

Teach, **"Last week we looked at the tools of Scripture and prayer cards. This week, we're going to look at a couple of others: listening to God and journaling."**

Chapter 29 (25 min)

1. Begin with question 1. Help people stick to what Paul relates in his story.
2. On your flip chart, ✍ draw a rough sketch of the chart on page 246 with just the titles "Word Only," "Word and Spirit Together" and "Spirit Only" filled in.
3. Move into question 2. ✍ List what we miss under "Word Only" and the results of this.
4. Under "Word and Spirit Together," ✍ write observations from question 3.
5. For question 5, ✍ list what we miss under "Spirit Only" and the results of this.
6. Record ✍ people's observations from John (question 6) in "Word and Spirit Together." Ask, **"Why do we need the Word of God and the Spirit when we pray?"**
7. Move through questions 7-9, focusing on how you learn to listen, and what this looks like.

Chapter 30 (25 min)

1. Open up by asking, **"Does anyone regularly journal?"**
2. To the person(s) who says yes, ask, **"Do you mind us asking you questions?"** If you have his or her okay, ask, **"How does it help you? What kinds of things do you journal about?"**
3. Discuss questions 1-3.
4. Ask your group to share what they learned through their journal experiences in question 4.

Prayer Suggestions (15 min)
Choose one of the following:

• Are you more "Spirit Only" or "Word Only"? What does it mean for you to pray the third way? If you are more "Word Only," be still before God. Wait for him to speak by bringing things to mind. If you lean toward "Spirit Only," pray through one portion of Psalm 119.

• Print out a psalm of your choosing onto a page, leaving space to reflect on it through journaling. Distribute a copy to each person.

WEEK 12

Introduction
Teach, **"We've finished looking at the tools of Scripture, prayer cards and journaling. This week, we're going to look at a picture of praying in the nitty-gritty of real-life. Then we will take a bigger look at our unfinished stories — from God's vantage point."**

Chapter 31 (25 min)

1. Ask, "If someone were to walk into your real-life praying, what would they describe?"
2. Move on to question 1. ✎ Draw on your flip chart two columns: "Seek for experience with God" and "Invite God into my experience," and record people's observations.
3. For questions 2-3, help your group get a feel for how earthy this prayer time is.
4. Close by asking, **"Go back to how you described your real-life praying. How does Paul's experience encourage you?"**

Chapter 32 (30 min)

1. Before asking question 1, ✎ draw the following chart:

What happened to Israel	What God did for Israel/us
1. Temple is destroyed	
2. Jerusalem is destroyed	
3. The walls are torn down.	
4. The kingdom is gone.	
5. The people are deported.	
6. Unbelievers brought in to resettle.	
7. The glory departed from Israel.	

2. Have people read Psalm 137:1-6. Ask, **"If you were Jewish at this time, what would you have been thinking? What would have been going on for you?"**
3. Ask question 2, reading aloud Haggai 2:1-3, etc.
4. For question 3, return to the chart, filling in the second column with people's answers.
5. Ask question 4, leaving people space to talk.
6. Conclude with question 5.

Prayer Suggestion (15 min)

Pray for one another's unfinished stories.

Homework

Remind people to reflect on one or two things they would like to take away from the study, and one tool they would like to try over the next month.

WEEK 13

Reflection

    1. Teach, **"What an adventure this has been! Today, we're going to reflect on what God has taught us, and celebrate together!"**

    2. Invite people to share one or two things they would like to take away from this study, and one tool they would like to try out the next month.

Prayer Suggestion (10 min)

Thank and praise God for what he has done among you.

LEADER'S GUIDE FOR 18 WEEK SCHEDULE

How to Prepare
- Read chapters ahead of time. As you read, highlight or underline a couple of things that were especially helpful or meaningful to you.
- Work through the discussion questions.
- Familiarize yourself with the questions from the leader notes. All questions you're to ask are in **bold type**. Find a way to easily reference these questions while leading.
- We recommend you purchase a flip chart, because it allows you to review previous lessons. This ✍ symbol in the guide indicates what you are to write on your chart. Whenever possible, write out charts and questions beforehand.
- Plan on each study taking about 60 minutes. This includes prayer.

How to Lead
Leading a study in prayer is an adventure, led by the Spirit. As a leader, what matters most is loving people in your group and bringing them to Jesus. This study guide is meant to be a tool to that end, but not the end in itself. As you lead, take time to listen to people, to enjoy them. Resist the temptation to rush ahead, finish people's sentences, or fill uncomfortable silences. At the same time, you want to avoid discussions that wander off topic. Gently return your group to the questions, saying, "That's interesting, but would you mind if we talked about that later? Let's move on to..." As you lead with an ear to the Spirit's convicting and comforting, you will discover the beautiful stories God is weaving in people's lives. What a privilege!

The best way to keep in tune with these stories is through prayer. At the end of each study, even if you have to cut your discussion short, devote ten minutes to prayer—practicing what you learned. During this time you may want to have people pair up to foster more intimacy, or stay together. This is up to you. (If your group is mixed gender, we encourage you to split up according to the same gender.) At the end of each discussion section are suggestions for prayer. We do not mean for each of these suggestions to be followed, but for you to pick one or two suggestions that are best for your group. For instance, in Week 10, people in your group discussion may have been struck by praying for a specific change in our culture. Rather than read each of the prayer suggestions, invite people to focus on praying for our culture. You're just following the Spirit's lead. If it's not clear what you should do, give people a couple of choices.

When you pray, we recommend that you set in place guidelines, and post them where they are visible.

Including Newcomers to Prayer

So many people are hungry for God. When Jesus tells the story of the Pharisee and the tax collector praying, it's the tax collector's prayer that the Father hears. Ironically, when it comes to bringing our friends to Jesus, sometimes our prayers get in the way. The longer we pray, the more spiritual we sound. The more we can intimidate. Then, without realizing it, we miss the short quieter prayers of our friends, "God help me! I'm a mess!" It isn't complicated leading people to Jesus. It's just a matter of creating space where we pray more simply, and allow our real selves to meet our real Father.

We welcome your feedback. Please email us at info@seeJesus.net.

WEEK 1

Introduction (10 min)

Welcome people to your group and explain the following:

- **Read chapters ahead of time. As you read, note passages that were especially helpful or meaningful to you.**
- **Work through the discussion questions from this schedule.**
- **Each week, we'll set aside time to pray.** Explain the below guidelines.

Prayer Guidelines

Our intent behind these guidelines is simply that they be helpful in directing you to pray. You may want to make your own or modify what we have. Whatever you do, we recommend you type it up, and put it somewhere visible where people can see it each week.

- No gossip. Sadly, we can be notorious for disguising our gossip through prayer requests! But let it not be.
- Limit your prayer to what you can say in a breath. This way our prayers will feel more like conversation and less like monologues.

Chapter 1 (25 min)

1. Start by asking participants, **"What are your frustrations with prayer?"** Invite people to be candid; this is not the time for Sunday school answers! ✍ Write everyone's answer on the flip chart.

2. Follow this up by discussing questions 2 and 6. Being vulnerable yourself will help others to be vulnerable.

3. Read "Ashley's Contact" (pp. 17-18).

4. Invite people, **"Talk about a time when God specifically answered a prayer. What happened?"**

Chapter 2 (25 min)

1. Ask, **"Which aspect of 'the praying life' spoke to you most? Why?"** Encourage people to be brief – you just want to get a sense of what impacted them.

2. Explain, **"We'll get to unpack some aspects of a praying life this evening, but probably not all. Let's look at the first aspect. How is prayer like having a meal with good friends?"**

3. Follow this up, reading the last two paragraphs from page 20. Ask, **"What happens when we make prayer our focus?"**

4. Continue reading from page 21, the fourth paragraph: "You don't experience God; you get to know Him. You submit to Him. You enjoy Him. He is, after all, a person." Refer back to question 6 from chapter 1 and ask, **"What does it mean that God is a person? Let's go back to our phone call with a person—God. Why might our view of God's personhood affect our conversation with him? Which of the experiences in our prayer might be different if we view God as a person?"**

5. End by discussing questions 9 and 10.

Prayer Suggestion (10 min)

Thank God for one aspect of a praying life from chapter 2.

WEEK 2

Introduction

Ask, **"What are some words that describe children—how they behave, talk, play, look?"**

Chapter 3 (20 min)

1. Lead people through questions 1-2. When you get to 2, ✍ write the "Coming Messy" chart (found on p. 19 of this guide) on your flip chart, and fill it in with people's own observations, using their words.

2. Sit on questions 3, 4, and 5. These are the heart of this chapter, and in fact, the very heart of prayer. How we come to God mirrors the gospel. People must understand that God wants them to come messy. This is the good news of the gospel. He will have us no other way!

Chapter 4 (25 min)

1. Jump into questions 1-2, further filling out what it means to come as a child to God.

2. In question 4, you want to leave people with a strong impression of what this widow was like, and the obstacles she faced. The more people think about her obstacles, the more they will be able to transition to thinking about their own pestering (question 5).

3. Discuss question 5.

4. At the end, describe how "playing" and "coming to God messy" are two sides of the same coin — coming to God as you are.

Prayer Suggestions (15 min)
Choose from one of the following:
- Practice coming to God messy and/or playing.
- Pester God in a childlike way.

WEEK 3

Introduction
Explain, **"Think of a time when you really wanted to get to know a person. Maybe it was your future wife, husband, an incredible mentor, a coach, etc. How did you get to know them?"**

Chapter 5 (20 min)
1. Read the first paragraph on page 43. Ask, **"Why did Jesus need to pray?"**
2. Discuss question 2. Understanding this will lay the foundation for the rest of the chapter.
3. Read together John 5:1-6. Ask, **"What do you observe about how Jesus focuses on this man? How can you tell that he is focused on him?"** ✍ Write down people's answers.
4. Immediately follow this up, and ask, **"How does it affect you that the Father loves you with the same one-on-one attention when you pray?"**
5. For question 4, ✍ record everything your group observes about how Jesus prayed.
6. Then, ask question 5, helping people to grasp what happens when we don't invest in relationships.
7. If you are meeting in a larger group, have people break up in groups of two to three. If your group is small, just stay together. Have people share their reflections on questions 6-7, and invite each person to pick a suggestion to try the following week.

Chapter 6 (25 min)
1. Read together Psalm 142, explaining that this psalm was written by David when he was in the cave (I Sam. 23-24), escaping King Saul's murderous intent toward him. Unpack your answers to questions 1-4, sticking to the Psalm as much as possible for your answers.
2. Invite people to share a situation in which they were helpless to act on their own and had to rely on others. These questions lay the groundwork for working through the central questions of this chapter: 5-7.

3. For questions 5-6, ✍ write people's answers on the flip chart.

4. For question 7, ✍ write out the chart from page 57 on your flip chart and fill it in.

5. Conclude your discussion with questions 8-9. People may feel more free to answer question 9 if you lead in being vulnerable. No one likes to admit helplessness!

Prayer Suggestion (15 min):

Choose one of the following:

• Take time to get to know God. Right now. Read a short passage of Scripture, and talk with him about what you see there. Ask him questions too.

• Where are you feeling helpless right now? As you share, instead of talking and giving advice, go directly to God praying for one another. Remember he likes messy.

WEEK 4

Chapter 7 (20 min)

1. Using your flip chart, ✍ write "What is poor in spirit?" across the top. Ask people questions 1 and 2, recording their answers on the chart.

2. Read aloud from Mark 10:46-52 and Luke 18:9-17. Ask, **"What makes blind Bartimaeus and the tax collector poor in spirit?"** ✍ Add their answers to the chart.

3. Ask, **"When Jesus tells the story of the tax collector and Pharisee, what connection does he make between the poor-in-spirit and repentance?"**

4. Ask question 5, inviting people to share personally.

Chapter 8 (25 min)

1. Explain, **"In this session we'll be looking at the first of two things that can paralyze us in prayer: worry."** Discuss people's responses to the first question, by just highlighting the second portion. There will be a time later when people can talk about their anxieties more in depth when they pray.

2. Ask, **"Think of a situation right now where you are experiencing anxiety. What is your natural response to this?"**

3. Jump into questions 2 and 3, filling out how anxiety is warped, and how prayer is so much better.

4. Read together Psalm 131, and together respond to question 4.

5. Ask, **"Does this mean we shouldn't go after complex things? How might it be possible to go after complex things with a child-like heart?"**

6. Ask: **"How can you check your heart? What are the warning signs of it becoming prideful?"** (Hint: what is this chapter about?)

Prayer Suggestions (15 min)

Pray like Bartimaeus and the tax collector — if possible go into separate rooms in case you want to get noisy. You can:

• Pray about your list of sinful tendencies that can drive you to pray continually. Repent of these poor-in-spirit style. Then, ask God to use these patterns to make you more like Bartimaeus.

• Explain to God your anxieties. Ask him to help you, remembering that he is God and you are not.

WEEK 5

Introduction

Ask, **"Have you ever felt like you're on a rough stretch of road with no end in sight, or like you've been let down just once too often? Last week we learned to call out in childlike trust to our Abba Father when we are feeling weak or helpless. This week we'll look at the alternative: to become defeated or cynical."**

Chapter 9 (45 min)

1. Explain, **"Before we see cynicism's effects, we need to see what it is."** Jump into questions 1-3, helping people to describe cynicism and how it tempts, subtly corrupting.

2. For questions 4 and 5, draw the following chart on the flip chart.
✍ Write people's responses to questions 4 and 5 in the first "Fruit" row. For the next row ask, **"What drives us to cynicism?"** [naïve optimism] **"What core beliefs are at the center of naïve optimism?"** ✍ Record people's thoughts. Then ask, **"What drives us to a praying life?"** [faith]

	Cynicism	A praying life
Fruit		
What drives us to:		
Core beliefs about God & people:		

3. Explain, **"Let's look at Psalm 23 to understand the core beliefs that are the center of faith. What is true about people in this psalm? What is true about God?"** ✍ Record observations on the chart.

4. Ask, **"How is faith different from naïve optimism?"**

5. Continue with question 8. The more you help your group observe how God brought meaning to David's story, the more easily they will

see God bringing meaning to their own stories. ✍ To help people grasp this, draw the following chart. Record people's answers in the corresponding spaces.

	David	You
How God brings meaning to:	{Say, **"Let's list what God does in Psalm 23."**}	{Ask, **"How do you see God bringing meaning to your story as he did for David?"**}

Prayer Suggestion (15 min)
Name before each other and God specific things that you are cynical about. Then spend time naming different attributes of God, focusing on his character.

Cynicism Homework (5 min)
Read the homework assignment on page 36, and pass out a piece of paper to each person for recording. Explain that you will debrief this next week.

WEEK 6

Introduction
Debrief people's cynicism homework. Ask, **"What did you learn about yourself? About cynicism?"**

Chapter 10 (30 min)
1. Ask the group, **"Which of Jesus' first four cures grabbed you — being warm but wary, learning to hope, becoming like a child, or having a thankful spirit?"**
2. Discuss the two most popular cures, based on their responses.
3. Lead the group on to cure five, "Cultivating Repentance," discussing the questions in this section.

Chapter 11 (15 min)
1. Based on questions 1 and 2, say, **"Let's go back to the cynicism exercise. As you prayed to see more of Jesus, what happened?"**
2. Ask question 3. Make it more personal too, asking, **"How did looking for Jesus specifically help you with your struggles with cynicism?"**

Prayer Suggestions (15 min)
Choose one of the following:
• Pray together aloud, naming the ways in which you are two-faced. Ask God to change you.
• Read through Psalm 23, and thank God for how he is good to you,

for how you have recently seen the presence of Jesus.

WEEK 7

Introduction

Teach, **"Last week we looked long and hard at cynicism and how to follow Jesus out of it through cautious optimism and a childlike, hopeful, grateful and repentant spirit that looks for evidence of His presence and power. This week we're going to look at why asking is hard, and what mindset our Father wants us to have when we ask."** Ask, **"To start off, think of a time you were filled with wonder as a child. What happened? What was it like?"**

Chapter 12 (40 min)

1. Begin by pointing to the diagram on page 105, explaining how secularism sees the world.
2. Ask questions 2 and 3.
3. Briefly summarize the story of Dana and her son Luke (pp. 108-110).
4. Ask question 4.
5. Read from the first paragraph on page 110, and ask questions 5 and 6.
6. As you discuss question 7, be prepared to share your own situation.
7. After a few minutes of sharing, recap the problem of a secular worldview — the false dichotomy that it sets up.
8. Ask questions 8 and 9.
9. As you ask question 10, help people to be as concrete as possible.
✍ Write people's answers on the flip chart.

Prayer Suggestion (15 min)

Pray through question 10.

WEEK 8

Chapter 13 (15 min)

1. Ask question 1.
2. Have someone read aloud 2 Chronicles 6:14, 18-21. Explain the context of the passage.
3. On your flip chart ✍ draw the following chart. Fill in the chart with people's observations from the passage.

Infinite	Personal

4. Ask question 4. If time permits, ask question 5.

Chapter 14 (25 min)

1. Explain, **"Let's talk frankly about what we perceive as spiritual and unspiritual requests. Give me some candid examples."** Using the flip chart, ✍ write out the people's responses. Then ask question 1.

Spiritual Requests	Unspiritual Requests

2. Ask question 2, filling out the "why" behind this false dichotomy.
3. Ask question 3. Have someone read aloud from Matthew 7:7-11.
4. Work through questions 4-5. Read aloud from pp. 123-124.
5. Discuss question 6, citing the 2nd and 3rd paragraph on page 125.
6. Conclude with question 7.

Prayer Suggestions (15 min)

Invite people to split up into pairs and do one suggestion of the following:

- What details would you like to ask God about that you hadn't considered before? What are your pajamas and spilled milk? Ask God to provide for your needs, explaining to him the details.
- What areas of your life do you want to control rather than give to God? How do you think he might mess it up? Be honest with God, explaining your hang-ups, and ask him to change you, to help you trust him.

WEEK 9

Introduction

Teach, **"Last week we talked about this radical concept of an infinite-personal God. Before Christ, most cultures other than the Jews believed in tribal gods who were limited and distant, not infinite and personal. The Jews believed that the infinite God of the universe was concerned about individuals—unheard of! And the idea of the incarnation, the infinite God with us, was completely radical! They believed, as we do, that God interacts with history. But even though we say we believe this, prayer is still hard for us. In today's lesson, we get to ask ourselves if we really believe that the extravagant promises of Jesus about prayer are real. What do they mean? What are the implications? And how does that affect our praying life?"**

Chapter 15 (20 min)

1. Work through question 1, reading the verses aloud, and ✍ writing down what makes people nervous.
2. Move quickly through question 2, then read James 4:2-3.

3. Review the path of "Good Asking" illustrated on page 132. Ask, **"What is dangerous about each side?"**

4. Ask, **"Which side do you tend towards?"**

5. Discuss Jesus' two antidotes to wrong asking in question 4.

6. Ask question 5, encouraging people to become askers.

7. Write ✍ a list of what we don't ask for (question 6).

8. Discuss questions 7 and 8.

Chapter 16 (25 min)

1. Ask question 1, but don't spend too much time here. The idea is to remind people of last week's lesson – that it is good to ask and that asking leads to bigger asking.

2. Lead the group into question 2, ✍ drawing the following chart and filling it in with people's observations.

	Abiding Person	**Not Abiding Person**
How do they respond to Jesus as King?		
How do they ask God for help?		
How do they involve the body of Christ in their lives?		

It is important that people grasp what happens when we isolate praying from the rule of Jesus, from the body of Christ (his church). Even more significantly, we want people to understand what abiding looks like as we pray and interact with the body of Christ.

3. Flesh out questions 3 and 4.

4. Invite people to reflect on question 5 together. You'll likely only have time to listen to two people share. As people share, avoid the temptation to give advice. Instead, pray either now or at the end of your time.

Prayer Suggestions (15 min)

Choose one of the following:

• Brainstorm for five minutes about what you would like God to do for you. Pray out of your brainstorming.

• Think of a situation in which you need wisdom. Write down the details, your questions, etc. What would it look like for you to ask God for wisdom, with an abiding heart? How would you ask? Would you surrender your will? How would you involve the body of Christ?

WEEK 10

Introduction

Teach, **"Paul writes, 'At the center of self-will is me, carving a world in my image. At the center of prayer is God, carving me in his Son's image' (p. 156). This week we'll be looking at how change can happen in people, beginning with us and our self-will."**

Chapter 17 (20 min)

1. Discuss question 1.
2. Skip question 2. But before asking questions 3 and 4, say, **"Now keep this person in mind from question 2, but for confidentiality, don't say who they are when answering these next questions."**
3. Discuss questions 5-7.
4. If you have time, talk together about one thing in our culture that you want to see God change. What do you want God to do? ✍ Make a list together.

Chapter 18 (25 min)

1. Discuss question 1 to get a sense of what self-will can look like.
2. Move on to question 2. On your flip chart, ✍ write, "Doors Jesus closes to self-will." Draw a copy of the chart on page 159.
3. Read Matthew 5:21-26, 27-30, 38-48. Say, **"Let's name all the doors Jesus closes here."** Next ask, **"What does he call us to give up when it comes to relationships?"**
4. Go on, reading Matthew 6:1-8, 16-34. Ask, **"Which doors does Jesus close to self-will in this passage? What is he asking us to give up?"**
5. Read Matthew 7:1-7. Ask again, **"Which doors does Jesus close to self-will in this passage? What is he asking us to give up?"**
6. Ask question 2.d.
7. Move into questions 3-5. Question 6 will be a prayer suggestion.

Prayer Suggestions (15 min)

• Privately, think of a person you would like to see change. On your own, pray for change to come. Then ask God to show you how you might be sinning like him or her. Close by giving thanks for that person.
• Pray for change to come in one particular way in our larger culture.
• Go back to the door that "hurts" the most to close. This is the door Jesus wants to close. Invite Jesus to do that, admitting to him the silliness of insisting that this door stay open. Then invite Jesus to open the door to prayer.

WEEK 11

Introduction

Teach, **"Last week we looked at how our self-will stands in opposition to God's work in us and in others. This week, we're going to look more deeply at how God works in others through us when we enter our Father's story."**

Chapter 19 (20 min)

1. Reflect together on questions 1-3, giving people a sense of the stories God unfolds when we pray.

2. Go into questions 4 and 5, looking at how our methods of changing others fall short.

3. For question 6, ✍ write on the flip chart, "What prayer does that other methods can't" and record people's observations.

4. Conclude with question 7. Question 8 will be a prayer suggestion.

Chapter 20 (25 min)

1. Summarize the Guatemala story from pages 173-177.

2. Ask questions 2 and 3, ✍ recording responses on your flip chart.

3. Wrap up with question 4.

4. Optional: consider asking someone in your group to share about how God has shown his love for them in spite of difficult role models.

Prayer Suggestions (15 min)

Choose to pray from one of the following:

• Reflect on the story God is telling in someone you love. How are you coming alongside of God and the story he's telling? Are there ways you are getting in the way? Pray to him, asking for insight into this.

• Paul writes, "If a ship is off a few degrees, it is imperceptible at first, but over time it becomes a vast distance. I was praying to prevent the distance of a heart gone astray" (p. 166). Think about one of your kids or someone else close to you, who you love as Paul loved Emily. What bend in his/her heart troubles you, frazzles you? What can you pray for him/her in response to this? Privately pray for this.

WEEK 12

Introduction

Teach, **"We've been talking about how God reveals the story he is telling in our lives. But what if, like Paul and Jill, we don't like our story? Yes, we can see that God is doing something, we just don't like what he's doing. We want to change a few chapters, rewrite the events, give it more or less drama, even delete some parts altogether. This week we'll be** talking about life in the 'desert'—this place of pain, disappointment and lack of our own resources. We'll be asking, 'Where is God in this place? What is he up to?'"

Chapter 21 (45 min)

1. Say, **"Turn to page 181 in** *A Praying Life.* **Take a couple of minutes to think about your desert."**

2. Ask question 2, using the questions to gently press into people's particular deserts.

3. Roughly ✍ sketch (you may want to do this beforehand) Paul's desert charts of despair, denial and determination (pp. 181-183). Discuss question 3, encouraging people to elaborate on specifics.

4. Read Genesis 15:1-6 and 16:1-6 and work through question 4.

5. Brainstorm all the good things God does in the desert – that he can't do anywhere else. ✍ Write people's ideas on the flip chart.

Prayer Suggestion (15 min)

Are you in the desert right now? Share in your group (as you feel comfortable) and let your group pray for you.

WEEK 13

Introduction

Teach, **"Paul writes, 'When we are in the middle of the desert, we feel like God is absent. We long for God to show himself clearly, to make sense of the mess.' (p. 189) This week, we'll be looking at these times when it feels like God is absent."**

Chapter 22 (40 min)

1. Say, **"Let's first look at how God lingers at the edge,"** and discuss questions 1-3.

2. For question 4, have people read the Scriptures and answer the corresponding questions.

3. Afterwards, ask, **"So, what does God grow in us through waiting?"** ✍ Record people's answers on the flip chart.

4. Discuss question 5.

Prayer Suggestion (20 min)

Reflect on what God has grown in you, by lingering at the edge. Savor Psalm 63, and thank him for loving your soul more than life.

WEEK 14

Introduction

Teach, **"Last week we looked at living in the desert — this place of pain, disappointment, and lack of our resources. This place where God so profoundly meets us. This week, we will see how God weaves hope and the gospel story into our lives, causing our desert to bloom into wonder."**

Chapter 23 (15 min)

1. Begin with question 1, helping people flesh out the fruits they see in their lives.

2. Help participants to think positively by asking, **"How would you be different if you really believed you were living in your Father's story?"**

3. Ask questions 2 and 3.

4. Ask question 4. This focuses on what is most challenging for many, *actually* staying in the story, continuing to be engaged. Ask, **"How are you tempted to disengage from the story?"**

5. Question 5 is great for encouraging people who are struggling to stay in the story.

6. Finish with question 6.

Chapter 24 (20 min)

1. Discuss question 1, encouraging people that they can dream big because God is big.

2. Ask question 3, helping people to see what can seem like a stone might really bread. Ask, **"Are there areas in your life where you have dreamed big before God, but feel you have a stone?"**

3. Ask questions 4-7. As you reflect on these, help people to feel a sense of the wonder, the real wonder they will experience when they see God bring their story together.

Prayer Suggestions (15 min)

Choose one of the following:

• Think through the list of three things (p. 201) that help us live in our Father's story: 1) Don't demand the story go your way. 2) Look for the Storyteller. 3) Stay in the story. Which of these challenges you the most? Pray for one another accordingly.

• How do you see God's craftsmanship in the story he is writing for you? What patterns/themes are emerging? How is he developing your character? Take time to reflect, thanking him for what he reveals.

• Take turns dreaming big before God. After each person dreams, pray with him or her for those dreams.

WEEK 15

Introduction

Teach, **"This week we're going to look at what happens when we live in the gospel story — in sync with our Father's world. Then, we'll look at the place of tools in helping us to pray."**

Chapter 25 (30 min)

1. Discuss question 1. ✍ Write down people's answers, highlighting the key themes. This exercise will help them answer question 2 more easily.
2. Ask question 2.
3. For question 3, ✍ list all the blessings.
4. Ask question 4. Invite people to think of specific times when God has brought meaning to suffering through working out his gospel story in their lives. ✍ Record what God did.
5. Discuss the first part of question 5, helping people see that living in the gospel story (1) anchors us to our real source of love, the Father, and (2) helps us to live connected to our world while in sync with our Father's world.

Chapter 26 (15 min)

1. Lead with questions 1-2. For question 2, ✍ record people's answers on your flip chart.
2. Move quickly into questions 4-6, giving people a sense of why systems can be helpful and what pitfalls to avoid.

Prayer Suggestion (15 min)

Praise God for ways in which your life resembles the gospel story.

WEEK 16

Introduction

Teach, **"Last week we talked about how we're all disabled and need help. We don't need to be afraid of systems – we use them all the time for things we care about! This week we'll be looking at several tools we can use to help us pray, specifically prayer cards and Scripture."**

Chapter 27 (25 min)

1. Before you meet, ✍ write the verse references in question 2 on a flip chart. Leave room between them for responses.
2. Discuss question 1.
3. For question 2, assign each group member a verse to read. After each person reads, ask – **"What phrases are used to describe what the Word of God is or what the Word of God does?"** ✍ Write their

answers on your chart.

4. After hearing all the answers, point to the chart and ask, **"Which ones give you confidence in the effectiveness of using God's Word in prayer?"**

5. Finish by debriefing prayer cards by asking questions 3 and 4. Affirm that this may work for some people, but not others. The point is to experiment in order to find the tools that work for you.

Chapter 28 (20 min)

1. Read together Mark 4:26-29. Sketch the following chart, leaving only the column titles and numbers. Invite people to compare and contrast the farmer with how we pray. Ask, **"What does the farmer do first, second and third? What do we do?"** As people answer, fill in the chart.

2. After people share their thoughts, explain how the farmer is just the opposite of us: we first WORK, then WATCH things fall apart, and then ASK when we give up. He first ASKS, then WATCHES God weave the story, and then WORKS alongside God.

How We Usually Pray	How the Farmer Works
1. We attack the problem [WORK]	1. He plants the seed of thoughtful praying. [ASK]
2. We watch things fall apart. [WATCH]	2. He watches and waits, looks for God's story. [WATCH]
3. Resort to prayer last minute. [ASK] Frustration, miss the story.	3. Recognizes the harvest; works in partnership with God. [WORK]

3. Ask question 2.

4. Conclude by discussing questions 3-4.

Prayer Suggestions (15 min)

Choose one of the following for your group:

• Make a prayer card. Think of a situation or someone you'd like to pray for, and find Scripture you'd like to use in praying. Feel free to use the examples on pages 227-231 in *A Praying Life*.

• When did you recently approach a problem the "usual way"? Remember the farmer and retrace your steps, planting seeds of thoughtful prayer.

WEEK 17

Introduction

Teach, **"Last week we looked at the tools of Scripture and prayer cards. This week, we're going to look at a couple of others: listening to God and journaling."**

Chapter 29 (25 min)

1. Begin with question 1. Help people focus on what Paul relates.
2. On your flip chart, ✍ draw a rough sketch of the chart on page 246 with just the titles "Word Only," "Word and Spirit Together" and "Spirit Only" filled in.
3. Move into question 2. ✍ List what we miss under "Word Only" and the results of this.
4. Under "Word and Spirit Together," ✍ write observations from question 3.
5. For question 5, ✍ list what we miss under "Spirit Only" and the results of this.
6. Record ✍ people's observations from John (question 6) in "Word and Spirit Together." Ask, **"Why do we need the Word of God and the Spirit when we pray?"**
7. Move through questions 7-9, focusing on how you learn to listen, and what this looks like.

Chapter 30 (20 min)

1. Open up by asking, **"Does anyone regularly journal?"**
2. To the person(s) who says yes, ask, **"Do you mind us asking you questions?"** If you have his or her okay, ask, **"How does it help you? What kinds of things do you journal about?"**
3. Discuss questions 1-3.
4. Ask your group to share what they learned through their journal experiences in question 4.

Prayer Suggestions (15 min)

Choose one of the following:

• Are you more "Spirit Only" or "Word Only"? What does it mean for you to pray the third way? If you are more "Word Only," be still before God. Wait for him to speak by bringing things to mind. If you lean toward "Spirit Only," pray through one portion of Psalm 119.

• Print out a psalm of your choosing onto a page, leaving space to reflect on it through journaling. Distribute a copy to each person.

Homework

Remind people to reflect on one or two things they would like to take away from the study, and one tool they would like to try over the next month.

WEEK 18

Introduction

Teach, **"We've finished looking at the tools of Scripture, prayer cards and journaling. This week, we're going to look at a picture of praying in the nitty-gritty of real-life. Then we will take a bigger look at our unfinished stories — from God's vantage point."**

Chapter 31 (20 min)

1. Ask, "If someone were to walk into your real-life praying, what would they describe?"
2. Move on to question 1. ✍ Draw on your flip chart two columns: "Seek for experience with God" and "Invite God into my experience," and record people's observations.
3. For questions 2-3, help your group get a feel for how earthy this prayer time is.
4. Close by asking, **"Go back to how you described your real-life praying. How does Paul's experience encourage you?"**

Chapter 32 (20 min)

1. Before asking question 1, ✍ draw the following chart:

What happened to Israel	What God did for Israel/us
1. Temple is destroyed	
2. Jerusalem is destroyed	
3. The walls are torn down.	
4. The kingdom is gone.	
5. The people are deported.	
6. Unbelievers brought in to resettle.	
7. The glory departed from Israel.	

2. Have people read Psalm 137:1-6. Ask, **"If you were Jewish at this time, what would you have been thinking? What would have been going on for you?"**
3. Ask question 2, reading Haggai 2:1-3 aloud, etc.
4. For question 3, return to the chart, filling in the second column with people's answers.
5. Ask question 4, leaving people space to talk.
6. Conclude with question 5.

Closing (20 min)
1. Teach, **"What an adventure this has been! Today, we're going to reflect on what God has taught us, and celebrate together!"**
2. Invite people to share 1-2 things they would like to take away from this study, and one tool they would like to try out the next month.

Prayer Suggestion (10 min)
Thank and praise God for what he has done among you.

ABOUT THE AUTHORS

COURTNEY MILLER SNEED lives in the Philadelphia area with her three young daughters and her husband Ian. She has written and enjoyed leading Bible studies while on staff with InterVarsity Christian Fellowship, and continues to do so with seeJesus. Though her quiet times are frequently noisy, she delights in learning to live in a good God story.

CYNDI ANDERSON has been a leader of women and children's Bible studies for nearly 20 years. Her background in Christian retail, publishing and curriculum development has given her passion for teaching God's word and connecting with people of all ages in a life-changing way. She has two adult children and eight grandchildren. She and her husband Lanning serve the Lord in their church in Williamsburg, Virginia.

PRAYERLIFE SEMINAR

This seminar is for badly praying Christians who are tired of struggling with prayer. Participants learn step-by-step how to begin a rich, private life of prayer. Seminar format works well in a retreat setting. The book, *A Praying Life*, is based on the principles first developed in the PrayerLife Seminar.

BOB ALLUMS, PRAYERLIFE DIRECTOR

REFLECTIONS ON THE SEMINAR:

"It was very freeing. I feel excited about prayer—it's no longer a restricted activity, but a place where I can be honest before God."

"I loved the down-to-earth honesty in PrayerLife about what keeps us from praying. I received intensely practical advice and applications. The prayer times were great."

**For more information on a
PrayerLife Seminar or Retreat
call 215.721.3113 or
visit seeJesus.net/Events.**

PRAYERLIFE RESOURCES

DVD
Filmed live before a church group, the four disk series presents Paul Miller teaching through all eleven lessons. **$60.00** [4 disk set]

AUDIO CD
Perfect for listening to in your car, this CD set is the complete audio version of the DVD study. **$30.00** [4 disk CD set]

—Disk One
1. Why Is Prayer So Hard?
2. Becoming A Child Of Your Father

—Disk Two
3. Begin Early With Your Father
4. Helplessness: The Key To Effective Praying
5. Ask Your Father Anything

—Disk Three
6. Entering Your Father's Story Through Prayer
7. Learning To Listen To Your Father

—Disk Four
8. Put The Word To Work
9. Prayer Work
10. Thanking God
11. Repentance and Intercessory Prayer

LEADER'S MANUAL
A perfect companion to the DVD series. This Leader's manual provides additional questions and teaching notes to supplement and enhance your group study. [96 pages]
$10.00 ea. [1-9] • **$9.00 ea.** [10-19] • **$8.00 ea.** [20+]

PARTICIPANT'S MANUAL
The Participant's Manual follows the outline of the DVD series leaving room for the student to take notes. [96 pages]
$7.00 ea. [1-9] • **$6.00 ea.** [10-19] • **$5.00 ea.** [20+]

SPECIAL LEADER'S PACKAGE
Included in this package is one Leader's Manual,
20 Participant's Manuals, plus the DVD set.
Special Price: $160.00

**To order call 215.721.3113
or visit seeJesus.net/Store.**

HOW DO YOU LOVE WHEN YOU GET NO LOVE IN RETURN?

HOW DO YOU LOVE without feeling trapped or used?

HOW DO YOU LOVE when you have problems of your own?

THE PERSON OF JESUS: A STUDY OF LOVE is a 48 lesson small group study that introduces a Christ so personal, so rich in love that participants are captivated heart first. The winsome insights of author Paul Miller, coupled with an energetic, interactive format, lead participants to discover answers from the Bible for themselves.

Five Units (can be taught stand-alone or in sequence):
- Compassion—Jesus moves into other people's worlds.
- Honesty—His commitment to truth balances his compassion.
- Dependence—He relies on his Father to shape His love.
- Faith—His faith energizes his love.
- Passion—His death is at the heart of his love.